Twenty Studies

for Bassoon

Albert Vaulet

Revised by H. Voxman

HAL•LEONARD®
CORPORATION
7777 W. BLUEMOUND RD. P.O. BOX 13819 MILWAUKEE, WI 53213

T0050633

Twenty Studies for Bassoon

Albert Vaulet

Revised by H. Voxman

Nº 1   Allegretto e staccato

© Copyright MCMLVIII by Rubank, Inc., Chicago, Ill.

Nº 2 Moderato legato

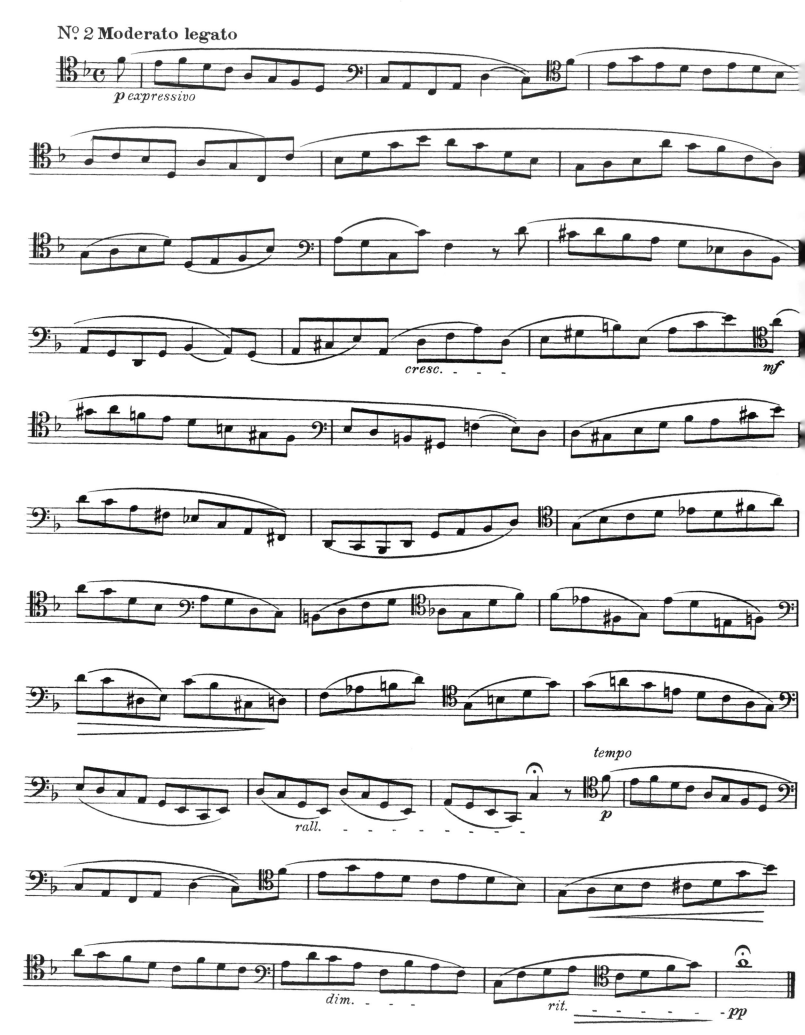

Nº 3 Vivo leggiero

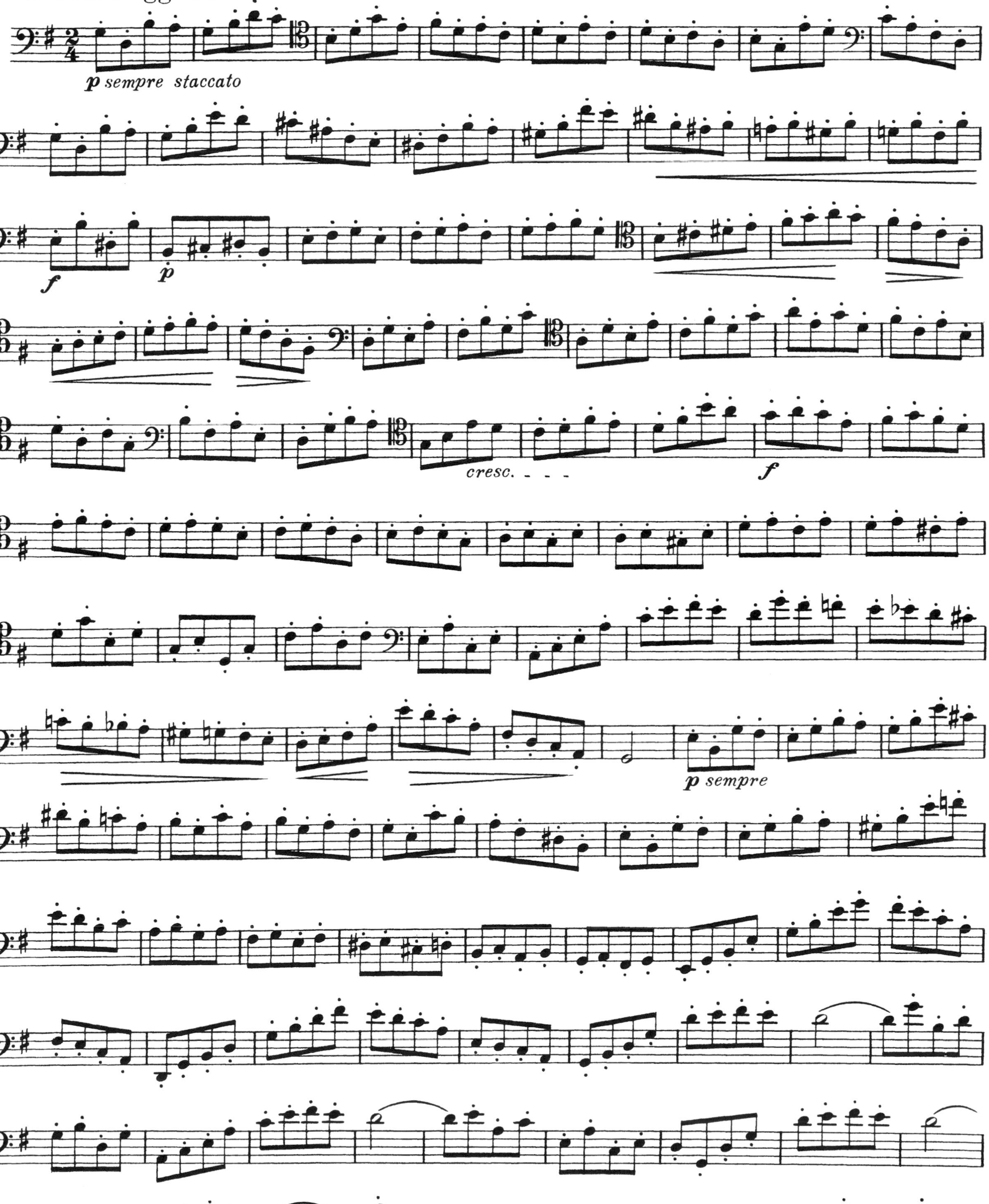

666-22-PL

6

Nº4 **Allegretto legato**

N.º 5 Allegro con brio

N.º 6 Rondo grazioso

N.º 7 Scherzo vivace

N.º 8 Allegretto con moto

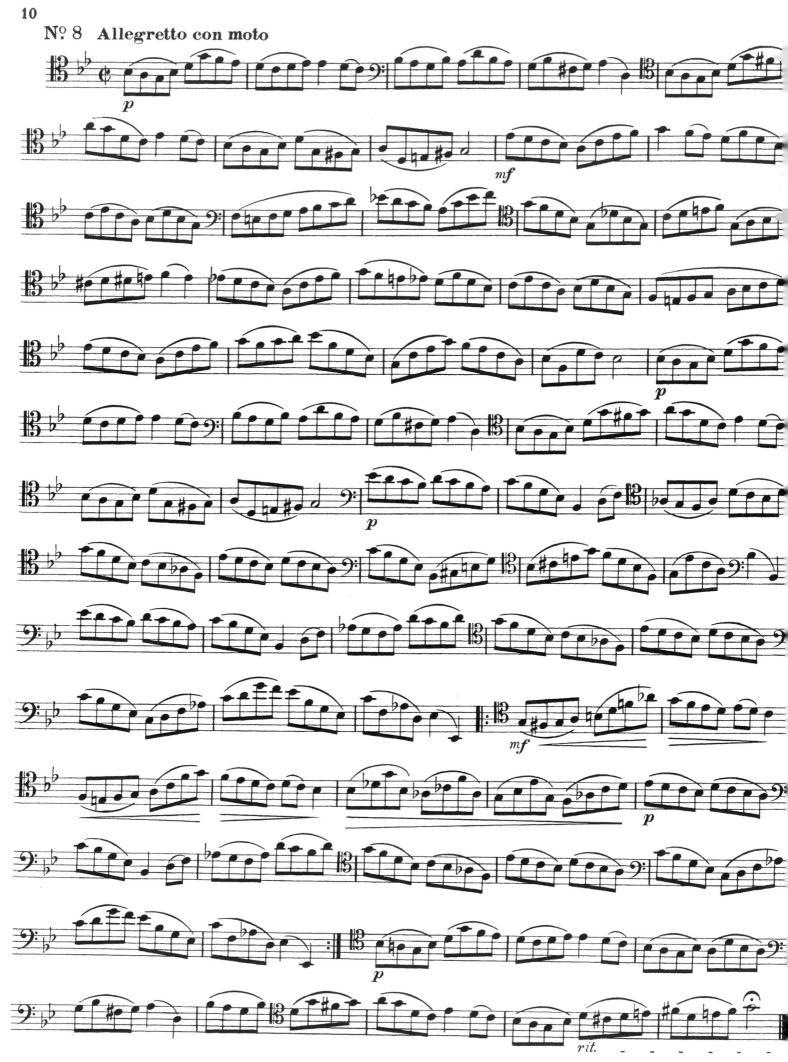

Nº 9 **Allegretto**

Nº 10 **Moderato**

Nº 11 Moderato marcato

Nº 12 Andantino con espressione

Nº 13 Tempo di Polacca

Nº 14 Andantino gracioso

Nº 15 Allegro moderato

1ere fois legato
2e fois staccato

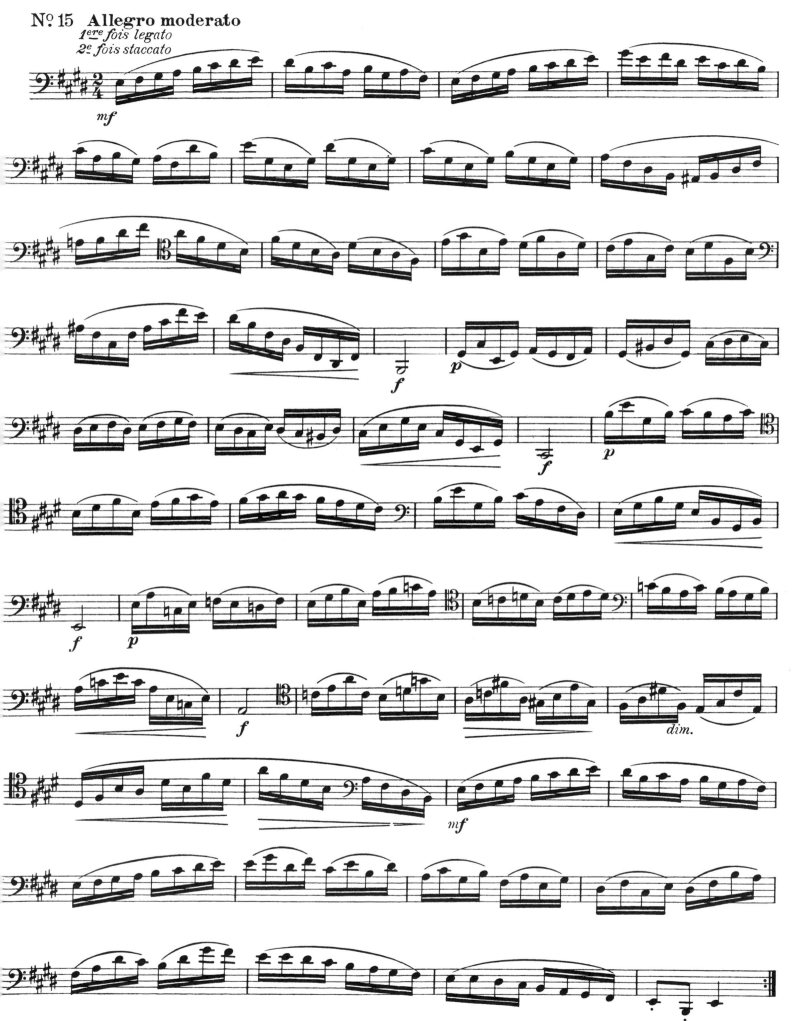

Nº 16 **Larghetto e Tarentelle**

Vivo giocoso

19

Nº 17 Allegro energico

Nº 18 **Allegro**

Nº 19 **Allegro marcato**

Moderato con moto

Nº 20